W9-AAM-583

CENTRALIA M.S. SCHOOL
901 Johnson Rd.
Centralia, WA 98531

Math in the Real World: How Deep Sea Divers Use Math

Chelsea Clubhouse
An imprint of Chelsea House Publishers
132 West 31st Street
New York NY 10001

Library of Congress Cataloging-in-Publication Data
Arroyo, Sheri L.
        How deep sea divers use math / by Sheri L. Arroyo; math curriculum consultant, Rhea A. Stewart.
            p. cm. — (Math in the real world)
        Includes index.
        ISBN 978-1-60413-611-1
        1. Mathematics—Study and teaching (Elementary)—Juvenile literature. 2. Scuba diving—Juvenile
        literature. 3. Deep diving--Juvenile literature. I. Title. II. Series.
    QA135.6.A774 2010
    510—dc22   2009018413

Developed for Chelsea House by RJF Publishing LLC (www.RJFpublishing.com)
Text and cover design by Tammy West/Westgraphix LLC
Illustrations by Spectrum Creative Inc.
Photo research by Edward A. Thomas
Index by Nila Glikin

Photo Credits: 4: OAR/National Undersea Research Program (NURP); Woods Hole Oceanographic Institution; 5: OAR/National Undersea Research Program (NURP); 6: iStockphoto; 8: Reinhard Dirscherl/Photolibrary; 10: Norbert Eisele–Hein/Photolibrary; 12: © José Antonio Hernaiz/age footstock; 16: Courtesty of Blue Water Divers/© Edward A. Thomas; 17: © Elvele Images Ltd./Alamy; 18: NOAA/NOAA PMEL Vents Program; 20: Kimmo Hagman/Photolibrary; 22: EPA/Region10 (Seattle) Dive Team; 23: Courtesy of Brenda Konar; 24: U.S. Navy photo by Mass Communication Specialist Senior Chief Andrew McKaskle; 26: © British Antarctic Survey; 27: Courtesy of Gayle Dana.

Printed and bound in the United States of America

Bang RJF 10 9 8 7 6 5 4 3 2 1

MATH IN THE REAL WORLD

How Deep Sea Divers Use Math

By Sheri L. Arroyo

**Math Curriculum Consultant: Rhea A. Stewart, M.A.,
Specialist in Mathematics, Science,
and Technology Education**

CHELSEA
CLUBHOUSE
An Imprint of Chelsea House Publishers

Table of Contents

Answers and helpful hints for the You Do the Math activities are in the Answer Key.

Words that are defined in the Glossary are in **bold** type the first time they appear in the text.

What Is Deep Sea Diving?

With a jump off the edge of a boat, deep sea divers enter another world. There is much to explore, since oceans cover more than 70 percent of Earth's surface. Many types of scientists study the oceans. There are also people who dive to do their jobs underwater—or dive just for fun. These people all use math before, during, and after their dives.

This man uses a JIM suit for a deep dive.

Zones of the Ocean

Since the world's oceans are all connected, scientists often talk about "the ocean" (meaning all of them). They divide the ocean into "zones," or levels, depending on how deep the water is. Water pressure increases as the ocean gets deeper. Divers need different equipment to handle the pressure at different depths.

Some divers wear only **wet suits**, masks, and air tanks on their backs so that they can breathe underwater. They are called **scuba** divers. They can dive to a depth of about 130 feet. Other divers climb into a JIM suit to dive deeper—as deep as 1,200 feet. The JIM suit is named after diver Jim Jarrett. It is a heavy metal suit with a big helmet that protects divers from the water pressure deep in the ocean.

Submersibles are small submarines that carry people very deep into the ocean. One type of submersible, named *Alvin*, can carry up to three people and can dive to 15,000 feet. Another submersible, named *Trieste*, once dived to more than 35,000 feet deep.

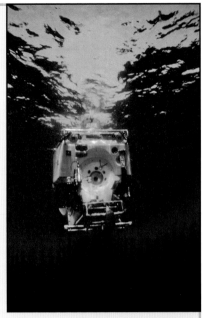

The *Alvin* submersible can go as deep as 15,000 feet below the surface.

You Do the Math

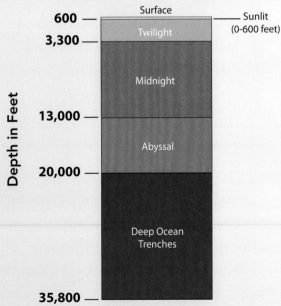

Zones of the Ocean

Depth in Feet

600 — Surface
Twilight
3,300 —
Midnight
13,000 —
Abyssal
20,000 —
Deep Ocean Trenches
35,800 —

Sunlit (0-600 feet)

Diving to the Depths

Look at the Zones of the Ocean chart to the left. It shows the names of the zones and how deep the water is in each one. In which zone is each of these divers:

1. Scuba diver at 60 feet below the surface

2. *Alvin* submersible at 14,000 feet

3. Diver in JIM suit at 1,200 feet

Scuba Diving in the Sunlit Zone

The sunlit zone extends from the surface of the ocean down to a depth of about 600 feet. Especially near the surface, sunlight brightens the water. Most animals and plants that live in the ocean live in the sunlit zone. The sunlit zone is where scientists study **coral** reef **habitats**, with their brightly colored fish and corals. It is also where **recreational divers** and underwater photographers usually spend their time.

A diver enjoys the brightly colored corals and fish in this reef.

Getting Ready to Dive

Divers need some special gear to dive in the sunlit zone. They need a mask, a wet suit, and a scuba unit that includes one or more tanks filled with oxygen, so that they can breathe underwater.

Divers prepare for a dive by studying tables of numbers that tell how many minutes a person can safely dive at different depths. In the table, each depth is written as a number followed by FSW.

FSW stands for "feet of salt water." So the number 40 FSW means a depth of 40 feet below the surface of the water.

The deeper the dive, the shorter the time a diver can safely stay down. Your body absorbs a gas called nitrogen when you dive. After a dive, it takes time for your body to release the nitrogen. If you do not release the nitrogen properly, you can get very sick. That's why there are time limits for safe dives. The table below shows the maximum dive time at different depths.

Maximum Dive Times	
Depth	**Time Limit**
40 FSW	150 minutes
50 FSW	80 minutes
60 FSW	50 minutes
80 FSW	30 minutes
100 FSW	20 minutes

You Do the Math

How Long Can I Dive?

Use the table above to answer these questions:

1. For how many minutes can you dive at 40 FSW?

2. For how many more minutes can you dive at 50 FSW than at 100 FSW?

3. What is the **difference** in time limits for 50 and 60 FSW?

4. For how long, in minutes, can you dive at 50 FSW? How many hours and minutes is this equivalent to? Remember, there are 60 minutes in an hour.

How Far Can I See?

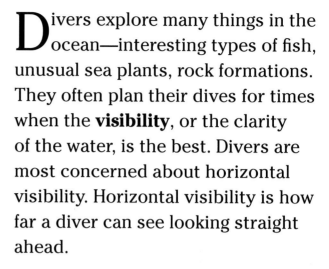

Divers explore many things in the ocean—interesting types of fish, unusual sea plants, rock formations. They often plan their dives for times when the **visibility**, or the clarity of the water, is the best. Divers are most concerned about horizontal visibility. Horizontal visibility is how far a diver can see looking straight ahead.

What Affects Visibility?

Several things can change the visibility of ocean water. For example, on a cloudy day, a diver won't be able to see as well underwater as on a bright sunny day. Visibility can change at different times of the year as well. This is because ocean temperatures affect the clarity of the water.

To help them pick the best time of year for a diving trip, divers study ocean temperature and visibility charts. The

This diver uses a flashlight to see better underwater.

charts show usual water temperatures and visibility at certain times of year.

Many people like to go diving in the coral reefs around Bermuda. Bermuda is a group of islands located 600 miles east of North Carolina in the Atlantic Ocean. The bar graph below shows how the water temperature and horizontal visibility usually change from month to month in Bermuda. Temperatures are shown in degrees **Fahrenheit** (°F).

Time of Year and Visibility

Look at the bar graph. About how many feet of horizontal visibility are there in January? About how many feet of horizontal visibility are there in August? What can you conclude about how ocean temperature and visibility are related?

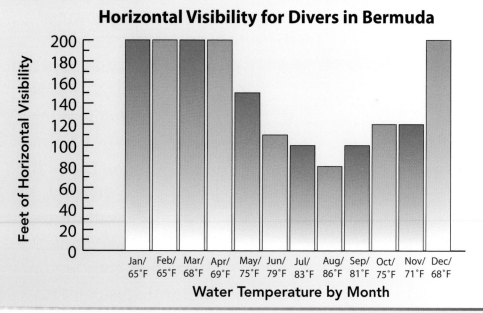

Horizontal Visibility for Divers in Bermuda

Diving into the Deep

Deep sea divers need to know about water temperature. This is not just because water temperature affects visibility. Knowing water temperature is also important because it helps divers to know what equipment they need to stay warm.

Dive Temperature

How warm the ocean is at the surface depends on where you are on Earth and what time of year it is. For example, in January, the temperature of the surface of the ocean can be a warm 90°F near the equator and a chilly 28°F in the Arctic. The water on and near the surface is warmed by the sun. In the deeper ocean, where the sun's rays are weaker or can't reach at all, the temperature drops quickly. Wherever you are on Earth, the deeper you dive, the colder the water gets.

Divers lose body heat when they are in water that is colder

For a dive in the chilly waters off Norway, in northern Europe, this diver's suit includes a hood and gloves.

than their body temperature—which is about 98°F. When they dive, divers have to be careful to avoid **hypothermia**, a condition in which body temperature falls dangerously low.

Divers use different kinds of wet suits to keep warm. Each kind is made of a certain type of fabric to keep divers warm in different water temperatures. Also, some wet suits are lined, and some come with a hood, vest, boots, and gloves. Even the best wet suits, though, won't protect divers if the water is cold enough. The table below shows what kind of wet suit to use in different water temperatures.

Water Temperature and Wet Suit	
If the water temperature is:	**Choose:**
78°F or above	Spandex wet suit
76°F or above	Unlined thermoplastic wet suit
72°F or above	Lined thermoplastic wet suit
60°F or above	Foam Neoprene wet suit with hood, vest, boots, and gloves

You Do the Math

Wet Suits

Use the table to help you answer the questions.

1. For a dive into 77°F water, what kind of wet suit should you wear?

2. For your dive trip to Bermuda in January, you are expecting a water temperature of about 65°F. What kind of suit should you use?

The Pressure Is On!

There is a blanket of air around Earth called the atmosphere. At **sea level**, 14.7 pounds of air presses down on every square inch of your body. This amount of pressure is sometimes called 1 atmosphere, or 1 ATM. Your body is used to a pressure of 1 ATM, and it does not feel uncomfortable.

Water is much heavier than air. When you dive, the weight of the water pressing on your body increases quickly as you go deeper. At a depth of about 33 feet, the pressure on your body is 2 ATM. That's double the pressure your body feels at the surface. This pressure pushes against the outside of your eardrums.

Equalizing Ear Pressure

Divers need to do what is called equalizing the pressure in their ears when they are descending (going deeper) into the ocean and when they are ascending (coming back up to the surface). One way divers do this is to pinch their nose and swallow. This allows air to move through

This instrument used by divers is called a depth gauge. It shows how far below the surface the diver is.

Pressure and Ocean Depth

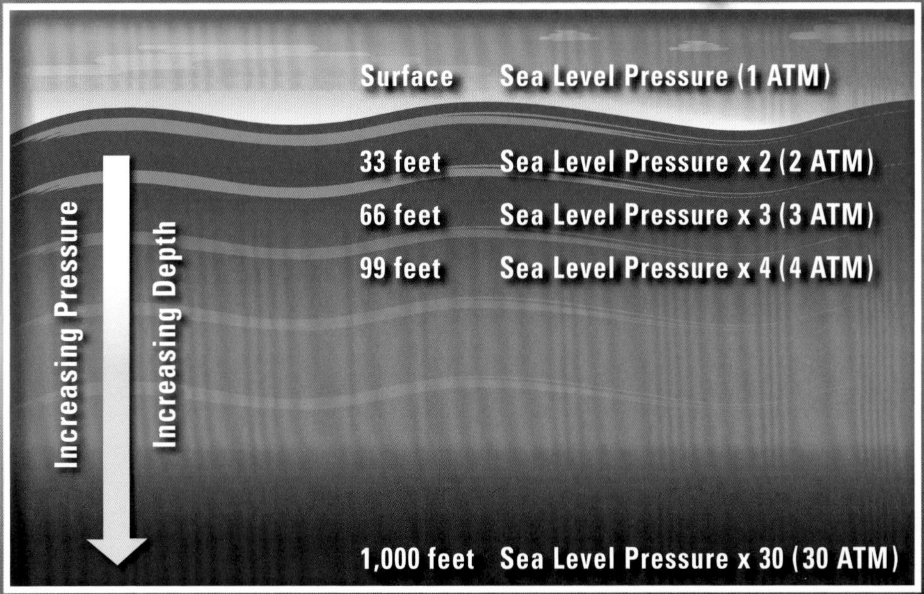

Surface	Sea Level Pressure (1 ATM)
33 feet	Sea Level Pressure x 2 (2 ATM)
66 feet	Sea Level Pressure x 3 (3 ATM)
99 feet	Sea Level Pressure x 4 (4 ATM)
1,000 feet	Sea Level Pressure x 30 (30 ATM)

Increasing Pressure

Increasing Depth

tubes inside the head to the inside of the eardrums, to balance the water pressure on the outside of the eardrums.

The pressure on your body increases rapidly as you dive deeper.

You Do the Math

How Often to Equalize

Divers often descend slowly—about 60 feet every minute, which is about 1 foot every second. These divers need to equalize pressure when they start the dive and then every 2 seconds (or every 2 feet) until they reach 30 feet. After 30 feet, divers who continue diving even deeper need to equalize pressure about every 3 feet. Use this information and the chart above to help you answer the questions.

1. If you dive to 33 feet, the pressure has doubled. How deep will you dive before the pressure doubles again?

2. You dive to a depth of 10 feet. How many times will you need to equalize the pressure in your ears?

3. You have descended to a depth of 66 feet. What is the pressure at that depth?

How Deep Is the Ocean?

Near land, the oceans are not as deep as they are far out at sea. The bottom of an ocean, sometimes called the sea floor, first slopes down gradually as you move away from land. Then the sea floor drops down sharply, and the oceans become much deeper.

Scientists have learned that most of the world's oceans are about 12,500–13,000 feet deep. In the deep ocean, though, there are mountains and canyons. So the depth can be very different in different areas. How do scientists figure out how deep an ocean is at a certain place?

By measuring how long sound waves take to get to the sea floor and back, scientists can calculate how deep the ocean is at that place.

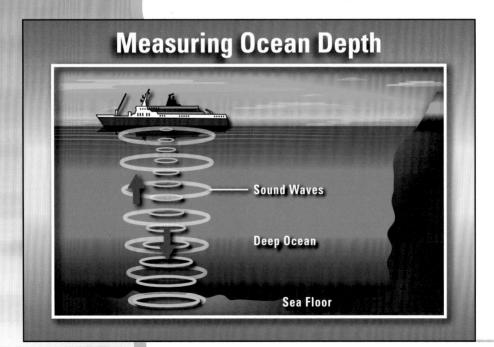

Measuring Ocean Depth

Sound Waves

Deep Ocean

Sea Floor

Measuring the Depth of the Ocean

Scientists **calculate** the depth of an ocean at a certain place by using devices called echosounders. Echosounders are attached to a ship. They send sound waves into the water. The sound waves travel to the sea floor and then bounce back to the ship. The echosounder measures the number of seconds that it takes for the sound to make the round trip.

Scientists know that sound travels in water at a speed of about 5,000 feet every second. So, to calculate the ocean depth in feet, they multiply 5,000 by the number of seconds divided by 2. They divide the number of seconds by 2 because the sound waves made a 2-way trip to the sea floor and back.

For example, to calculate the depth of the ocean at a place where the time measured by the echosounder was 4 seconds:

$$5{,}000 \times (4 \div 2) = \text{depth}$$
$$5{,}000 \times 2 = \text{depth}$$
$$5{,}000 \times 2 = 10{,}000$$

The depth is 10,000 feet.

You Do the Math

To the Sea Floor and Back

You're a scientist measuring ocean depth. Can you answer this question?

If sound waves take 8 seconds to travel to the sea floor and return to the ship, what is the depth of the ocean at that place?

How Much Air Will I Need?

A diver's breathing equipment includes a tank of **compressed air**, worn on the back. Compressed air is under high pressure, so that a lot of it can be squeezed into the tank. When the tank is full, the pressure may be 3,000 psi (**p**ounds per **s**quare **i**nch).

As a diver swims and uses up some air, the rest of the air in the tank can spread out, and the pressure goes down. After a diver has been swimming for 10 minutes, for example, the pressure may be only 2,800 psi. A gauge shows the diver the tank pressure. The lower the tank pressure, the less air the diver has left. Divers watch their tank pressure carefully. They want to make sure they have enough air to last for the entire dive.

Pressure gauges, such as this one, help divers know how much air they have left in their tanks.

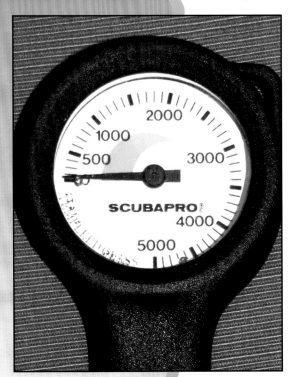

How Fast Air Is Used

How fast a diver uses up air depends on how far

below the surface the diver is swimming. At a depth of 33 feet, the pressure of the water on a diver—and the diver's lungs—is 2 ATM (twice what it is at the surface). A diver at 33 feet has to take twice as much air into his lungs with each breath as he would at the surface. This greater amount of air going into the lungs is needed to make up for the greater water pressure pushing in on the lungs. So a diver at 33 feet will use air from his tank twice as fast as someone swimming right below the surface.

A diver checks his gear before heading into the water.

At 66 feet, the pressure of the water is 3 ATM (3 times what it is at the surface). A diver at 66 feet uses up air at 3 times the rate of a diver just below the surface.

You Do the Math

How Long Will the Air Last?

A diver knows that his tank holds enough air for a 90-minute dive if he stays just below the surface.

1. If instead of staying at the surface, he goes down to 33 feet, for how many minutes will the diver's air last?

2. How many minutes will the air last at a depth of 66 feet?

Underwater Geologists

A **geologist** is a scientist who studies Earth and its natural features. Underwater geologists study soil, rocks, and landforms that are under the sea.

A group of underwater geologists is studying volcanoes on the sea floor. They are part of what is called the NeMO Project. NeMO stands for New Millennium Observatory. It is an observatory on the sea floor at Axial Volcano, an active undersea volcano off the coast of Oregon.

Project NeMO scientists use underwater vehicles without crews, such as the one below being lowered into the water. Operated by remote control from a ship, the vehicles can take samples of the soil or rock on the sea floor.

Volcanoes under the Sea

Scientists at Axial Volcano placed an instrument called a rumbleometer on the sea floor near the volcano to collect **data** on ocean temperature and depth.

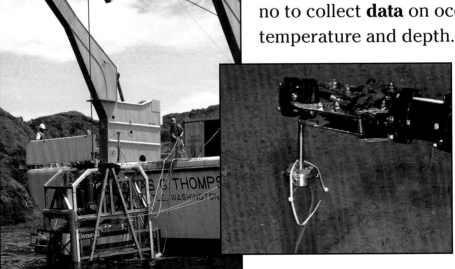

Then, there was a new eruption, and lava flowed from an opening in the sea floor right under the instrument. As the lava bubbled up, the instrument was lifted to a shallower depth. When the eruption stopped, the instrument moved back down.

The rumbleometer ended up sitting on top of a layer of lava that cooled and hardened on the sea floor. It was about 2 feet higher than when the lava flow started. The graph below shows data from the rumbleometer tracking its vertical (up and down) movement before, during, and after the volcanic eruption.

You Do the Math

Measuring Underwater Volcanoes

Look at the graph and see if you can answer these questions:

1. What is the rumbleometer's depth at 1 p.m.?

2. What is the rumbleometer's depth at 4 p.m.?

3. What is the difference between the rumbleometer's depth at 1 p.m. and 4 p.m.?

4. What is the depth at 5 p.m.?

5. How many hours does the data cover?

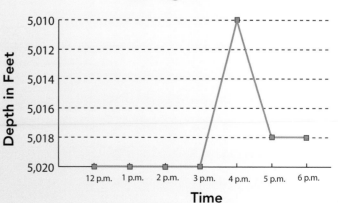

Rumbleometer Depth during Lava Flow

Exploring Shipwrecks

An underwater **archaeologist** is a scientist who learns about the past by studying sunken shipwrecks and their artifacts. Artifacts are objects made and used by people.

First, archaeologists dive down to the shipwreck to **survey** the site. They divide the site into small sections, so that they can make a careful and accurate record of where on the wreck artifacts are located. They use a measuring tape, stakes, and string to lay out a **square grid**. Next, they make a detailed copy of the grid on waterproof paper. They can accurately show on this paper copy the location of everything found on the wreck.

The Wreck of the *Boscawen*

An underwater archaeologist made a drawing like the one on page 21 of the wreck of the ship *Boscawen*. The ship was built in

A diver explores the wreck of a sunken ship.

The Wreck of the *Boscawen*

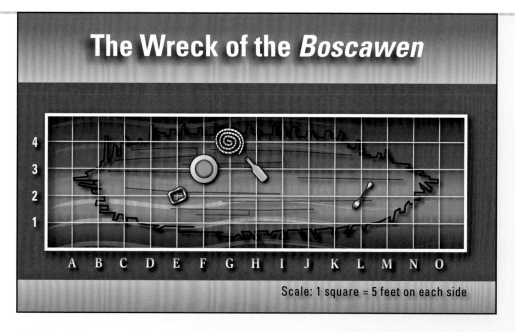

Scale: 1 square = 5 feet on each side

1759 to be used on Lake Champlain. Lake Champlain is located mainly in the states of Vermont and New York. Years later, the ship was abandoned, rotted, and eventually sank.

The archaeologist made a grid on the sketch of the *Boscawen*. Each point on the grid where two lines cross is named with a letter and a number. These are called the coordinates and written (letter, number). For example, the bottle is located at coordinates (H, 3).

You Do the Math

You Be the Archaeologist

Study the drawing of the square grid of the *Boscawen* wreck site. What are the coordinates for where the archaeologist found each of these artifacts?

1. Shoe buckle
2. Pewter plate

3. Spoon
4. Rope

How many feet long was the *Boscawen*?

Marine Biology

How many creatures live along the shoreline of the world's oceans? Scientist Brenda Konar is a **marine biologist**, and she is working to find out. Marine biologists study the oceans' plants and animals. The word "marine" can mean having to do with the ocean. Konar is working with other marine biologists on the Natural Geography in Shore Areas Project, or NaGISA. This project is studying marine life at locations along the shores of 51 countries.

Counting, Counting, Counting

The marine biologists are using a method called quadrat sampling to

This diver is setting up a quadrat to help count the number of plants and animals in an underwater study area.

estimate the number of marine plants and animals at each location. Here is how quadrat sampling is done: The habitat the scientists are studying is divided into a series of squares, or quadrats. Then, the plants and animals found in one quadrat are counted. Scientists can make an estimate of the total number of each kind of plant and animal in the entire study area by multiplying the number counted in one quadrat by the number of quadrats that cover the entire study area.

Scientist Brenda Konar, who lives in Alaska, takes a break during her research.

How Many Animals Live Here?

The marine biologists used 3-foot-square quadrats to count animals in shoreline areas. Look at the results below for three kinds of animals. Can you estimate how many of each kind is living in its entire area?

Animals in a Shoreline Area		
Animal	**Number in 1 Quadrat**	**Total Quadrats**
Starfish	6	7
Sea urchin	4	11
Snails	9	20

Diving for the Navy

A Navy diver welds a patch onto a warship.

Divers for the U.S. Navy are trained to do many different things. They do underwater repairs on ships and underwater construction projects. They are trained to dive to depths of up to 300 feet. They use special tools, watercraft, and remotely operated vehicles to get their underwater work done.

The Navy also tests new diving equipment. A special group, the Navy Experimental Diving Unit (NEDU), helped develop full face masks for divers and underwater voice communication. NEDU divers have tested scuba tanks of mixed gas, such as helium and oxygen, instead of compressed air. The use of mixed-gas tanks has made very deep dives possible.

Wet Suits versus Dry Suits

The deeper you dive, the faster you get cold. The colder you are, the more rapidly you breathe and the more air you use. Divers use special suits called dry suits for deep dives in cold water. The Venn diagram below compares wet suits and dry suits. The part of the diagram where the two circles overlap shows ways in which these kinds of suits are alike. The other parts of the circles show ways in which the suits are different.

You Do the Math

Comparing the Suits

Look at the Venn diagram. Then try to answer the questions.

1. What are three ways in which wet suits and dry suits are the same?

2. If you are planning to dive to a depth of 30 feet and the water temperature will be 50°F, which suit will give you the best protection?

3. If you are going to dive where the water temperature is 78°F, which suit should you use?

4. Why do you think a dry suit is better for colder temperatures?

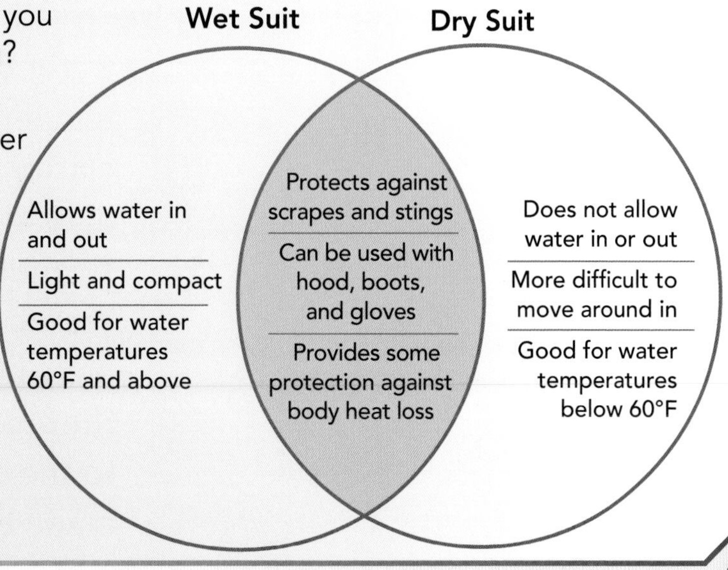

Wet Suit   **Dry Suit**

Allows water in and out
_____
Light and compact
_____
Good for water temperatures 60°F and above

Protects against scrapes and stings
_____
Can be used with hood, boots, and gloves
_____
Provides some protection against body heat loss

Does not allow water in or out
_____
More difficult to move around in
_____
Good for water temperatures below 60°F

Antarctic Research

The Southern Ocean surrounds the continent of Antarctica in the southern hemisphere. The climate is extremely cold, and parts of the ocean near Antarctica are covered with ice. However, the Southern Ocean is full of life—from tiny plankton to whales, seals, penguins, fish, and sea birds.

Even though the climate is so harsh, many scientists do research in Antarctica and the waters nearby. They study the region's climate, habitats, and animal life.

Instruments, Surveys, Data

Scientists have placed instruments in the water to continuously measure water currents, water temperature, and the clarity of the water. The data are sent back to scientists onboard research ships. Scientists have put recorders on the sea floor to listen to the sounds that are made by marine animals.

Scientists place instruments at various locations to gather data about the climate of Antarctica.

Some divers have gone underneath the ice in the Southern Ocean to map where krill are found. Krill are small shrimp-like animals that are an important source of food for larger animals, including whales. Divers worked in areas where the water temperature was only 28°F.

A diver works under the ice in the frigid water of the Southern Ocean.

How Cold Is It?

Scientists have measured the air temperature at several research bases in Antarctica. Temperatures were recorded in degrees **Celsius** (°C). The scientists calculated a **mean** temperature for each month by adding together all of the temperature

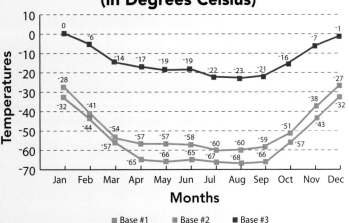

Mean Monthly Temperature (in Degrees Celsius)

Temperatures / Months

Base #1   Base #2   Base #3

readings for that month, then dividing the sum by the number of readings they had. The graph shows the monthly mean temperatures for a year at three research bases.

1. At Base #1, which month had the coldest mean temperature?

2. For June, how many degrees colder was the mean temperature at Base #2 than at Base #3?

3. At Base #3, what four months were the warmest?

If You Want to Be a Deep Sea Diver

Deep sea diving can be a hobby or an important part of a scientific career. Marine biologists, archaeologists, and geologists dive as part of their research. Some students who want to become scientists chose their area of study because they enjoy diving.

Learning How to Dive

Scuba diver training begins with classroom sessions, where you learn safety rules and the basics of diving. Then you will have a series of sessions in a pool, where you learn how to use all of the equipment. The last part of the training will be four open-water dives to depths between 15 and 60 feet. These dives are done under the supervision of a teacher. The open-water dives will complete your basic scuba diving training, and you will get a certificate saying you have successfully completed the course. There are advanced courses that further develop diving skills and train you to dive deeper or to dive at night.

Answer Key

Pages 4-5: What Is Deep Sea Diving:
1. Sunlit zone. **2.** Abyssal zone. **3.** Twilight zone.

Pages 6-7: Scuba Diving in the Sunlit Zone:
1. 150 minutes. **2.** 60 minutes (80 − 20 = 60).
3. 30 minutes (80 − 50 = 30). **4.** 80 minutes,
which is equal to 1 hour and 20 minutes.

Pages 8-9: How Far Can I See?
January: 200 feet. August: 80 feet. Visibility is
greater in colder water than in warmer water.
The water temperature is colder in January than
in August.

Pages 10-11: Diving into the Deep:
1. You need an unlined thermoplastic wet suit.
2. Foam Neoprene wet suit with hood, vest,
boots, and gloves.

Pages 12-13: The Pressure Is On!:
1. 99 feet. **2.** 6 times (1 time at the beginning of
the dive and then every 2 feet). **3.** 3 ATM.

Pages 14-15: How Deep Is the Ocean?:
20,000 feet, since 5,000 x (8 ÷ 2) = 20,000.

Pages 16-17: How Much Air Will I Need?:
1. 45 minutes (if a diver at 33 feet is using air
twice as fast, the air will last for one-half the time:
90 minutes ÷ 2 = 45 minutes). **2.** 30 minutes (if a
diver at 66 feet is using air three times as fast, the
air will last for one-third the time: 90 minutes ÷ 3
= 30 minutes).

Pages 18-19: Underwater Geologists:
1. 5,020 feet. **2.** 5,010 feet. **3.** 10 feet. **4.** 5,018 feet.
5. 6 hours.

Pages 20-21: Exploring Shipwrecks:
1. (E, 2). **2.** (F, 3). **3.** (L, 2). **4.** (G, 4).
The *Boscawen* was 70 feet long.

Pages 22-23: Marine Biology:
1. 42 starfish (6 x 7 = 42). **2.** 44 sea urchins
(4 x 11 = 44). **3.** 180 snails (9 x 20 = 180).

Pages 24-25: Diving for the Navy:
1. They protect against scrapes and stings. They
can be used with a hood, boots, and gloves.
They provide some protection against body heat
loss. **2.** Dry suit. **3.** Wet suit. **4.** It doesn't allow
water in.

Pages 26-27: Antarctic Research:
1. August. **2.** 39 degrees colder (the difference
between ⁻58 degrees at Base #2 and ⁻19 degrees
at Base #3). **3.** January, February, November,
December.

Glossary

archaeologist—A scientist who studies how people lived in the past.

calculate—To figure out the exact answer to a problem.

Celsius—A scale, or system, for measuring temperature. In the Celsius scale, water freezes at 0 degrees and boils at 100 degrees.

compressed air—Air that is held in a container under high pressure.

coral—A small sea animal that lives in large groups, or colonies, and makes a hard substance also called coral.

data—Information collected about people or things.

difference—The amount by which one number is greater than another number.

estimate—To get an answer that is close to the actual number or amount.

Fahrenheit—A scale, or system, for measuring temperature. In the Fahrenheit scale, water freezes at 32 degrees and boils at 212 degrees.

geologist—A scientist who studies Earth and its natural features.

habitat—The natural environment in which an animal or plant lives.

hypothermia—A condition in which body temperature falls dangerously below normal.

marine biologist—A scientist who studies the plants and animals living in the oceans.

mean—The sum of a group of numbers divided by the quantity of numbers in the group; also called the average.

recreational diver—Someone who dives just for fun or as a hobby.

scuba—One or more air tanks and other equipment worn by divers so that they can breathe underwater. Scuba stands for "self-contained underwater breathing apparatus."

sea level—A level that is even with the surface of the oceans.

square grid—A shape made up of rows of squares that are all the same size.

submersible—A small submarine that often carries one or more people down to the deep ocean.

survey—To look over and to measure.

visibility—How well things can be seen.

wet suit—A tight-fitting suit, usually made of a rubber-like material, that is worn by divers.

To Learn More

Read these books:

Covert, Kim. *Extreme Diving*. Mankato, Minn.: Capstone Press, 2005.

Lindop, Laurie. *Venturing the Deep Sea*. Minneapolis: Twenty-first Century Books, 2006.

Look up these Web sites:

Center for Ocean Sciences, Monterey Peninsula College, California
http://www.oceanCareers.com

Marine Science Careers, University of Delaware Sea Grant College Program
http://www.ceoe.udel.edu/seagrant/education/marinecareers.html

New Millennium Observatory
http://www.pmel.noaa.gov/vents/nemo/index.html

Oceans Alive!
http://www.mos.org/oceans/planet/index.html

Reef Environmental Education Foundation
http://www.fishcount.org

Smithsonian Ocean Planet Exhibit
http://www.seawifs.gsfc.nasa.gov/ocean_planet.html

Women Oceanographers
http://www.womenoceanographers.org

Woods Hole Dive and Discover Program
http://www.divediscover.whoi.edu

Key Internet search terms:

deep sea diving, marine biology, scuba diving, submersible

Index

About the Author

Sheri L. Arroyo has a master of arts degree in education. She has been an elementary school teacher in San Diego, California, for more than twenty years and has taught third grade for the past thirteen years.

DATE DUE

DEMCO 128-5046